APPREHENSIONS

OF WHAT-IS

APPREHENSIONS
OF WHAT-IS

Nature, Mystical Moments
and Understanding

by
Walt McLaughlin

Wood Thrush Books

Published by Wood Thrush Books
                27 Maple Grove Estates
                Swanton, Vermont 05488

ISBN 979-8-9881716-6-9

What is truth? Truth is something so noble that if God could turn aside from it, I could keep to the truth and let God go.

– Meister Eckhart

Introduction

As much as I hate to admit it, my perception of the world is not the reality of it. This is true of all human beings, by nature of us being human. And by "the world" I mean the universe at large as it passes through time — all that exists, ever existed, or ever will exist. What any of us knows about it is only a fraction of What-Is. The whole of it, what we call God or Nature, is beyond what any mere mortal can comprehend. Yet I still struggle to understand What-Is, as so many others do, while living as fully as I can in the here/now.

Several months ago, when the snow was gone but leaves had not yet sprouted from the swollen buds of trees, I backpacked a short distance into the Adirondack mountains. I made camp near a small pond then grooved with the wild as a steady rain fell. When the rain stopped, I started a small fire and kept it going until darkness enveloped the forest.

I snuffed out the fire then made my way down to the pond by headlamp before going to bed. A chorus of spring peepers, that had started singing when the rain stopped, grew louder and louder as I approached the water's edge. When I turned off my headlamp, the pond was barely visible.

I knelt on a large flat rock and splashed water into my face. The incessant high-pitched call of hundreds of small frogs in their mating frenzy rang in my ears. They were all around me. Water dripped from my beard. I looked up and saw the stars of the Big Dipper directly overhead. They seemed close enough to touch. I was immersed in the wild and completely overwhelmed by its otherness. That's when I felt it — the presence of the divine.

For lack of a better term, I call experiences like this mystical moments. They are encounters of the divine that render me speechless, that go beyond perception or understanding. In these fleeting moments, I *apprehend* What-Is without being able to *comprehend* it. Or at least that's what I think is happening. All I know for certain is that in such moments I temporarily forget myself and the whole universe unfolds in perfect unity. Then suddenly I am self-aware again and it is gone.

This is hogwash some will say, utter woo-woo. This is only my imagination running wild as I lose myself in an emotionally charged moment. Perhaps so, perhaps not. All I can say is that a glimpse of the whole of nature – the infinite – comes to me no other way.

Some people believe there is a rational explanation for everything, but it is impossible for me to comprehend What-Is intelligently, logically or rationally. I apprehend it in mystical moments that occur on rare occasions as I go about my life. Such moments always come when I least expect them — usually when I'm alone in the wild. They are not altogether thoughts or feelings, or even perceptions. They are apprehensions triggered by cognition and/or sensory input yet going way beyond that. It never lasts.

I am as much a mystic as I am a philosopher. I have spent my entire life trying to know the unknowable, that is, while trying to make sense of the world that I inhabit. Most people lean one way or the other, it seems, towards the left brain or the right, towards eastern thought or western, towards a rational understanding of things or an intuitive one, but I don't abide by that. I feel no need to choose between the concrete and the abstract.

As I wander through the woods, I am both in survival mode and chasing butterflies. I'm both practical and impractical that is. I'm careful about how I build a fire, maintain it, then put it out, yet I still hear strange sounds in the distance. Yes, I remain utterly rational even as my imagination runs wild. And my worldview reflects this. Anyone who has spent considerable time alone in the wilderness can relate, I'm sure.

Even though I penned the rough draft of this work in three days, it is the culmination of half a century of contemplation, woods wandering, reading and soul searching. This is a spiritual autobiography of sorts, as much as it is a philosophical treatise. Perhaps even more so.

In this succession of taut paragraphs, some of which could be considered prose poems, I have tried to sketch the relationship between us as thinking, feeling creatures and What-Is. I have tiptoed along that liminal edge between the knowable and the unknowable. I have kept it personal because encounters with What-Is *are* personal. They are deeply personal. Self and the divine other. It doesn't get any more personal than that.

Make what you will of this work but don't mistake me for some kind of guru. I'm just a guy muddling through this world, asking a lot of questions. Most of my questions don't have answers, but I think they're worth asking anyway. I hunger for truth, even though it eludes me. I try to make sense of what is seemingly absurd. I am God's fool. Perhaps my words have entertainment value and nothing more. Hard for me to say. I'll let you be the judge of that.

Walt McLaughlin
August 2025

APPREHENSIONS
OF WHAT-IS

Through our senses we know the world we inhabit. Science and reason expand our understanding of this world and the universe at large. Then there is What-Is, which is all this and more. Much more.

What-Is: All that is known and unknown. The particulars of the universe and the whole. All matter, all energy, all thought. Order and chaos. The laws of nature and the source of those laws. The immense fabric of existence, including everything that has ever existed or ever will exist. Reality in all its manifestations, along with its endless potential. That which is infinite and eternal.

I am a lost pilgrim, a seeker of the invisible. I hunger for an understanding of What-Is. Call me sorcerer, shaman, mystic, or madman. Or simply *Homo sapiens*. I have wandered through the wilderness for forty years, in hot pursuit of the infinite, only to remain bewildered. Now and then I catch a glimpse of Reality, but it vanishes like a desert mirage as soon as I approach. Or is this just my mind playing tricks on me?

Mystical moments. They come and go in the blink of an eye. In these incredibly brief glimpses of Reality time stops, my jaw drops, my mind opens wide, and I see that for which there are no words. In such moments I *apprehend* What-Is. Apprehended, yes, but not comprehended.

Caveat: Do not trust my words. I am just as ignorant about What-Is as you or anyone else. There is not enough room in the human brain for the infinite. I conceive only a fragment of it, which is not the infinite at all. And whenever I try to speak about the unspeakable, nothing comes out. Nothing, that is, that adequately describes What-Is. Sages remain silent, leaving such babbling to know-it-all fools.

All the philosophies and religions contrived by humankind fall short of the mark. We only fool ourselves when we expound our worldviews, saying: "This is it! This is the truth!" Those who agree with us are just as wrong. Those who disagree with us are not so easily fooled by our claims, yet they too have their illusions. We all *think* we can make sense of What-Is.

Staring into oblivion. The long desire. A hunger that cannot be satisfied. I feel this terrible and unrelenting urge to know What-Is, but I cannot know all there is to know. Even if I tried, there would always remain something unknown. The infinite cannot be grasped. And yet I can *apprehend* What-Is in mystical moments, however fleeting and unspeakable. I can directly encounter Reality. Or can I? Perhaps this apprehension is the ultimate delusion.

First encounter: The iced-over waterfall glistens in the moonlight while I sit in woody darkness, temporarily removed from the rest of humankind. The trickle of water still flowing beneath the ice breaks the searing silence. What is this feeling coming over me right now? I catch the sudden appearance of the unseen, but it is gone before I can make any sense of it.

Seekers beware! Contemplate the infinite long enough and you *will* go mad. I have. The human brain cannot conceive it. Infinite, endless, eternal... Do you really think you can make sense of that? Do you honestly believe that you can utter a few words or scribble a mathematical formula on a whiteboard that explains everything? Yes, that is madness.

"God" is the word we use when all language and thought has reached its limit. "Infinite," we say, objectifying What-Is. "God is infinite," we conclude, as if we have any clue what it is that we are talking about. Are these real words? Do they have any meaning at all? What exactly are we trying to say?

Yes, I can *apprehend* What-Is, but I cannot fully grasp it. And yes, this makes me apprehensive. I fear God. More to the point, I fear that which is unknowable. I fear *mysterium tremendum* – the Great Mystery that is nature. Science can only take me so far in my quest to understand it. Always there remains the frontier of knowledge. Beyond it lies the unknown.

Practical people stop thinking where science stops. Or they carefully inch forward as science does, theorizing perhaps, but doing their best to resist wild speculation. Or they simply turn back to what is concrete, rejecting all abstractions, as if Reality itself isn't riddled with abstraction.

Apprehensions of What-Is provide only one piece of useful information: that there exists now and will always exist some aspect of Reality that is beyond human understanding.

Like all human beings, I am a fundamentally absurd creature. I long for a complete understanding of myself, the world I inhabit, and the universe at large, so I dream up elaborate concepts to fill in the uncomfortable gaps in my knowledge. Time and time again, I reject the unknowable. What foolishness!

Why do I exist? I, *Homo sapiens*, long for a complete and irrefutable sense of life's meaning, so I invent meaning. That is the great folly from which all human tragedies emerge, including the tragic sense of life itself. I want the world to make perfect sense, so I fill in the blanks with gods, myths, logical theorems, or whatever. And yet the apprehensions of What-Is that come to me in mystical moments refute all these contrivances. Then I see Nature in both its mindboggling complexity and utter simplicity. Nature spelled with a capital "N" — that which underlies all things seen and unseen, What-Is. This astounds me, renders me speechless. What made me think I could ever make sense of it?

What-Is. Don't call it God unless you can accept that it is all things seen and unseen, all that ever has existed or ever will exist. What-Is is nothing like the anthropomorphic God that makes us feel good about ourselves: God made in our own image, the relatable God, God the father, God the king, etc. Better to remain silent. The word "God" falls woefully short of the mark. Even the word "Nature" isn't adequate. There are no words for What-Is, not even "What-Is." We really have no idea what we are talking about when we talk about the infinite.

"Why?" I shouted into the heavenly vaults, and in my incredible naïveté I expected an answer. That's how trouble begins: a heartfelt longing to understand the meaning and purpose of the universe at large and everything in it, including oneself. I was Adam taking my first bite from the tree of knowledge. In this acute self-awareness, I questioned everything. There's no turning back after that.

Mystical moments are not ecstatic realizations of truth, enlightenment, supernatural visitations, out-of-body experiences, communion with the divine, or anything generally associated with that incredibly misleading word "mystical." Is there a better turn of phrase for an apprehension of What-Is? Probably. But that too would be misleading, as all utterances about encounters with the unspeakable are.

God help me, I have no clue what I'm talking about when I talk about God, Allah, Brahman, Tao, Logos, Idea, the Absolute, or any other concept of ultimate Being. What-Is utterly astounds me. My apprehensions of it go beyond words, reason, mathematics, or perception. I am speechless before Reality, and incapable of fully comprehending it. I lose myself in its infinity.

Standing on the snowy shoulder of a steaming volcano, I gaze across the wild forest stretching before me in all directions. Then I am dazzled by that brilliant yellow orb climbing ever so slowly into the cloudless sky. Then I am awestruck by the presence of something divine, rendered completely self-less by it for a split second before returning to my senses. What did I just see? I keep asking myself that during the days, weeks, months that follow. Decades later, I still don't know.

There is order in the universe as surely as there is chaos. One implies the other. When someone tells me that everything is random, I can't help but laugh. Apprehensions of What-Is tell me otherwise. More importantly, I know that Nature exists. It is not just a figment of my imagination.

Two days deep into a sprawling wilderness, I leave the beaten path. Then I daydream through alpine meadows until I find a place next to a small stream to call home for a while. The next morning, I gaze upon the sheer rock wall beneath a cliff, seeing something there that I've never seen before: the wild incarnate, the face of all things seen and unseen. Then I walk in God's shadow the rest of the day, going nowhere, knowing nothing, shuddering before What-Is.

Wild reality. I didn't know what mountain lion tracks looked like until I saw that creature crouched above me on a ledge. Its presence spoke to me — volumes upon volumes of similar encounters between man and beast. Like this, the divine makes its appearance in strange ways. It comes when we least expect it.

Sometimes God is a burning bush. Sometimes a burning bush is just a burning bush. Sometimes it's impossible to tell the difference between the two.

I long for a place that I can never reach so long as I am still alive. A greater "I" awaits, but that terrifies me, reluctant as I am to surrender my small precious self to it. Yes, I am *self-ish*, and will remain that way until the day I die. It can't be helped.

Nature and only nature. The sky, the trees, the river — everything moves. Nature flows, along with everything in it. Eternal flux. All things change, transmute, become something else. There is nothing but change. I am horrified by this. My ego recoils from such terrible reality. It wants to exist forever. And perhaps it will as some part of the whole, but not as a self-serving ego. Not as something apart from the rest of nature. No, that can't happen. Nature, in the true meaning of the word, is an irresistible force, always changing, always taking on new forms.

Standing at the base of a cascading waterfall, ankle deep in its plunge pool, I can't see where this stream goes or how I am able to stand here. Does the stream go underground? If so, then what am I standing upon? "There must be a rational explanation for this," I tell myself, but I don't know it. I suspect the same can be said about What-Is. If I knew all there is to know, then What-Is would make perfect sense to me. But I am not omniscient.

That freight-train roar of wind across the barren alpine snowfield isn't something I can resist, so I emerge from the ravine where my friends and I have taken shelter for the night. I want to *feel* this elemental force. I step into it, pressing forward no more than a few yards before being blown off my feet. Then I crawl back towards the ravine as the wind's icy embrace rapidly strips away the heat from my body. I scramble back to safety, a much smaller creature than I was just a few minutes ago. I grossly underestimated the power of nature.

A cosmological humiliation. In a fit of temporary insanity, I honestly believed that I could venture one-way into the wilderness and become perfectly attuned to it like a holy man dressed in skins — one with God. But all the plants, animals, rocks, and stars started laughing at me. The entire universe laughs at my incredible arrogance, my self-involved determination to become more than just another creature bungling about in this world. I, *Homo sapiens*, am Nature's jester. I am God's fool.

The universe is greater than my idea of it. My concept of What-Is is woefully inadequate. Nature tells me daily how wrong I am, but I'm not listening. I shut out that noise, thinking I have a good bead on things, calling myself *Homo sapiens* — wise man. Yeah, right. Like I have any clue what is really going on.

Ensconced in a makeshift burrow next to a fallen tree, I hunker down before an unexpected mountain storm. I am too deep in this wild forest to get out before dark. The air turns cold. Rain becomes sleet then snow. The wind howls. In the first glimmer of morning light, I beat ice from my rain jacket and break camp. Then I dodge falling trees while following a raging stream down to the nearest road. The wind's ferocity is nothing personal, I assure myself, breaking ice out of my beard. It simply is what it is.

Hidden in plain sight, the ultimate reality of Nature eludes me. The particulars of it are easy enough to grasp, but the whole is beyond my comprehension. What is this phenomenon that I call Nature? What is the driving force that transforms chaos into order? I am astonished by it.

Deep in the trackless forest, I attempt once again to reach the summit of a remote mountain. A sheer rock wall prevents me from going any farther, until I find a narrow passage cutting through it. On top at last and looking down, I feel somewhat removed from the rest of the world. The bustling town on the horizon looks dreamlike and far away, as this mountaintop does from there. With my precious self stripped down to the bone, I make a small sacrifice to What-Is in this sacred place. Then I descend, never to return.

God exists; God does not exist. These are only foolish words uttered by creatures like me too full of themselves to see What-Is. Reality resists such scrutiny. None of our abstractions, rational or otherwise, can get near it.

On a rock breaking the water's surface in the middle of a sprawling lake, I stand at dusk with a companion as wild-eyed as I am. The moon arises, the sun sets, and ours is a planetary awakening. How easy it is to forget that we inhabit a blue sphere circling a star somewhere in the cosmos. I sense the divine everywhere, all around me. What made me think there is anything in nature that isn't holy?

Mystic, mysterious, mystifying. These words suggest a fuzzy apprehension of What-Is, but I never see it with such intense clarity as I do when I lose myself in mystical moments. Completely immersed in wildness, I see the whole of Nature. Reality stripped of all preconceptions. In this eternal now, I see without seeing. I see with a third eye. Then I snap back to a temporal existence, back to my precious self. Such encounters never last long.

It came to me in a dream – how arrogance would be my demise. I would slip from the high narrow ledge, thinking I could cross it, then slide all the way down into cold, dark waters below. Fully awake months later, I came upon that ledge and hesitated long enough to hear wild nature urging me to abandon my folly. I have listened to that voice ever since, heeding its sage advice as much as is humanly possible. Yet I remain God's fool.

Stark reality. Deep in the alder bush, I stalk a bear. Or is the bear stalking me? The moose bones scattered along the river's edge tell a terrible story. I read them, getting the message loud and clear. I, too, could go that way. I am *involved* with this wild world.

Question your most cherished beliefs long enough and they will vanish into thin air, leaving you naked before What-Is. Only then will you be fully alive.

What's the difference between a philosopher and a fool? What's the difference between an animal and an enlightened one? Nature does not discriminate. All things exist in the same four dimensions, except perhaps Nature itself. Not a difference of quality, but of degree. If I fully understood how evolution works, I would know the mind of God. But I have my thoughts, my abstractions instead. So much for loving wisdom.

Pagan fishing. As the biggest trout I have ever landed slips out of my hands and back into the drink, the hook still in its mouth cuts deeply into my finger. I rise to my feet, howling loud enough for the bald eagle flying past to take notice. Not that it cares. My blood splatters across the smooth stones underfoot in tiny explosions. In this moment, I arrive — the wild is no longer something alien to me.

The sun drew a circle around me as I tended a campfire, dipping below the northern horizon only briefly that night. That is how I, *Homo sapiens*, found my place in the universe. The world turns. The days come and go. The cycle never ends. And I am exactly where I should be — at home on a planet that spins like a top as it circles the sun.

What kind of beast am I, self-aware and always thinking, thinking? Furry creatures assure me that they too have some idea what's going on around them, that they too have some sort of consciousness. But I have all these abstractions, these words, these symbols of things both real and imaginary. Do I not eat, drink, sleep, and copulate like every other animal? Do I not breathe? How did I become such a cognizant creature? To what end? This is, to be sure, the greatest mystery of all mysteries.

Down by the stream rushing past endlessly, I hear wood elves conversing in the distance. It's only my imagination, of course — the sound of water animated in my head. Yet the stream talks to me all the same. It speaks a liquid language, punctuated by streambed rocks. I cannot decipher it, but I'm sure that I'd know all of Nature's secrets if I could. The stream does not lie any more than rays of sunlight or raindrops do.

Reason is my most powerful tool. With it I can decipher almost everything in nature. Everything, that is, except Nature itself – that irresistible force driving all things. So I declare the universe unknowable. Others conclude that the universe is utterly random, thus protecting their egos from the blinding glare of What-Is.

Campfire flames dance before my eyes, licking back the darkness that envelops me. These animate gases mesmerize. They suck all thoughts out of my head, replacing them with flashes of darkness and light, heat and cold, fiery movement and surrounding stillness. That is how they open me to What-Is. I stare unknowingly into the campfire, immersed in its elemental existence, completely here and now.

There was a moment, before the antibiotics kicked in, when I felt the cold hand of Death upon my shoulder. My doctor called it pneumonia. Microbes were having their way with me. My wheezing was a sure sign of serious trouble. I felt myself weakening, weakening... Now I have a rough idea what the end of me will be like.

The first time I raised binoculars to my eyes and saw that ghostly apparition in the night sky, I thought my mind was playing tricks on me. But the spiral galaxy Andromeda was exactly where my star chart told me it would be. Is that island universe really two and a half million light years away? Are there really a hundred billion stars in that nighttime smudge? Impossible! The early winter chill shooting through me felt like the frigid embrace of deep space itself. I couldn't get warm. Months later, I saw Andromeda and other more distant galaxies through a telescope and still couldn't believe my eyes. The vastness of the cosmos makes my head explode. I am told that the entire universe emerged from a singularity fourteen billion years ago. Suddenly science and religion have become indistinguishable. What am I to make of all this?

The divine is precisely that which holds all things together, creates order out of chaos, makes everything evolve. It's implied whenever I think or talk about the laws of nature. Do such laws really exist, or are they only figments of my imagination?

The key to understanding the laws of nature lies in the very concept of mind itself — what happens exactly whenever I think, talk, or imagine anything. What is this "I" that does the thinking, talking, and imagining? Am I only a figment of my own imagination? If so, then what's doing all this imagining? More to the point, how can even a single thought exist in utter chaos?

There is this small "I" that is me, then there is the greater "I" that is What-Is. What is the relationship between the two? Why does this small "I" exist at all? If I knew the answer to either one of these questions, I would know all there is to know. I would know the mind of God. But I haven't a clue.

I found a lost pond once by getting lost. I became so disoriented that I began to question my compass. Then the lost pond appeared. There were no trails to it or from it. And it was not properly located on my topographical map. When I left that pond, I became lost again, so I can't say with any precision where it is. Coming upon a woods road shortly thereafter, I then knew *exactly* where I was. But the lost pond remained lost. Now I wonder if I was ever really there.

God is precisely that which we cannot possibly conceive, as hard as we may try.

I call myself a pantheist for lack of a better word to describe what I believe about myself and the universe. But pantheism is no more real than any other *-ism*. When I say that God is Nature, I am only uttering words, desperately trying to make sense of What-Is. But I'd keep my mouth shut if I had any sense. Then people would think that I actually know something.

Honestly, I don't know how to be completely honest without discarding my pen and remaining silent. In my incredible arrogance I think, as most thinkers do, that I have a good bead on things. But I'm only groping about in the dark — just another wisefool. Pay no attention to me.

Poets know what philosophers do not, that words can be blathered into oblivion. This is especially true when we talk metaphysics. Empirically speaking, physics makes sense while meta-physics does not. Rationally speaking, we are limited by the chains of language — mathematics being one of them. We have no means by which we can get directly at What-Is. We can only talk around it.

In the Alaskan wilderness, I picked up an eagle feather, keeping it close at hand for days, thinking I could somehow tap its spiritual energy. Then I waded knee-deep into the frigid, fast-moving river, feather in hand, reluctantly letting go of it, watching the current carry it away. That was an important step on my long, unfinished journey towards accepting What-Is. Letting go.

Are you still listening to me? Have you heard anything I've said so far? Do you still cling to your most cherished beliefs? Do you think you have a good bead on things? In that case, then ignore my words. They are of no value to you. I have nothing to offer but a cloud of unknowing in the face of What-Is.

Gazing deep into the forest, I see only trees and more trees. Then suddenly I see something else. Seeing beyond seeing. Seeing everything and nothing. Seeing all Nature, What-Is. Lost in the moment. At loss for words. Utterly astounded. Then snapping out of it, I toss another stick on the campfire.

Deep in a wild forest, I acknowledge my own wildness. All nature is wild, including me. My domestication is only a temporary condition. The stars will have no part of it. Nor will the wind. Yet we domesticate other creatures, as well as ourselves. We domesticate everything we lay our hands upon. To what end? The wild will ultimately prevail. It is, after all, the will of God.

For many people, sex is the only wildness they allow themselves. They copulate like animals then spend the rest of their time pretending they are something else. It's almost as if they are ashamed of themselves, unwilling to have anything more to do with their own nature than that.

Full moon over a wilderness lake. Absolute stillness. I awaken to a profound silence. Eyes wide open, I listen for as long as I can before returning to the dreamworld. It's too much. I can only take Reality in small doses. I want wild nature to conform to *my* way of thinking, to *my* way of seeing things. But it has its own agenda, unbeknownst to me.

It's hard to return to my own kind after running wild in the forest for a week or so. It's hard to keep from screaming at the top of my lungs. What we call modern living is too much. Is *this* the price we must pay to interact with each other?

My canine companion knows as much as I do about nature. She knows as I know that not everything can be known. She is both wild and domesticated, and feels the tension between the two. Yet she is just as happy as I am to run wild in the forest for a while, to be *here and now*. The pleasures of domestic living can wait.

Do you really think that nature is an aberration, that it exists despite the will of God? Do you honestly believe that to be fully alive in this world — to eat, sleep, copulate and breathe — is some kind of sin? Are we incapable of any kind of *natural* holiness?

The evolution of the universe from inconceivably hot plasma to what it is today infers that life forms have not always existed. They began with a single existent transforming at some point from inanimate to animate matter *before* any kind of reproduction. This only stands to reason. So how did that transformation take place? What was it in Nature that invoked this incredible change?

We are told that the entire universe can be traced back to a spacetime singularity. How is that possible? More importantly, what got the ball rolling? What caused the universe to unfold? What eternal law of nature creates a universe, and from what exactly? When people say the word "multiverse," I laugh. They think they are dodging the divine by imagining more universes than this one. Yet *something* must be infinite for anything to exist at all.

Sometimes a thought can trigger a mystical moment. When we least expect it, when we are thinking in terms of science and science only, the divine suddenly appears out of nowhere. When we ask deep enough questions, it becomes unavoidable.

Deep in a wild forest, I stumble upon a creature sprawled across the trail and dying for no apparent reason. No tooth-and-claw reason, that is. Disease perhaps, or simply old age. Hard to say. But in its final life-spasms, I see my own destiny. I see the destiny of all living things. Death is inevitable. Yet life goes on without this or any other individual being in the world. I don't understand why. I don't know what all this living and dying is for – how it got started, why it is happening, or to what end. Life itself is a great mystery.

The bones of dragons haunt humankind. We find them buried deep in the earth. What are we to make of these bones? What prehistoric monsters dominated this planet before we came along? What will some future beings think when they stumble upon our graves? What stories will they tell each other to explain our bones?

There are mystical moments that conform to our preconceived notions about how spirituality works, then there are those that take us completely by surprise. No one expects to find God in a laboratory, much less in gnarled traffic, or on a sunny summertime beach. Such moments are supposed to occur in the desert or some other great wilderness, in some temple designed for spiritual awakening, or atop a mountain. Such moments are associated with dark nights, great storms, a profound turning inward, and long solitary journeys. Yet the divine is everywhere, everywhere.

Using a telescope, I find Sagittarius A in the night sky, just above the southern horizon, at the bottom of the Milky Way. There, I'm told, a massive black hole churns at the center of our galaxy. But I don't see it. There is nothing to see since light cannot escape from a black hole. Am I supposed to take such things on faith? The astrophysicist's math assures me that the black hole is there, but I still don't see it. Since it is a black hole, no information is forthcoming, other than the relentless tug of gravity. What other secrets is Nature keeping?

Because we have made God in our own image, we think the divine is intelligible. I prefer the word "Nature" when contemplating the Great Mystery. That way I *know* it is beyond my comprehension.

In every way of seeing or thinking about the world there are preconceptions. Even in the most rigorously logical way of thinking there are givens. What do you *assume* to be true? Give that a second thought. Question that.

Tautology. One equals one. Circular thinking. In every belief system — and all we have are belief systems — the proof always comes back to an assumption. I am I, for example, assumes I. But to understand What-Is, I would have to know both I and not I, being and not being, God and not God. Is that even possible considering the limited amount of grey matter between my ears?

Let's create artificial intelligence capable of thinking what we cannot think. Ah, but the machine can only crunch the information that we put into it. No synthesis there. Nothing new. Only computations at the speed of light. A machine's thoughts will always be binary.

Wandering through the stars one night, while staring into the eyepiece of a telescope, I lose my way. I become so disoriented that I no longer know which way is up. Then it occurs to me that "up" doesn't really exist in space. It is relative to a fixed point, and the only fixed point I have is me on the planet that I inhabit. But neither this planet nor I will last forever. What fixed point will there be once we are both gone? Does it matter?

I walked with God, but God was nowhere to be seen. I talked to God, but the only response was silence. Clearly God does not exist then, because my senses do not register it. And my senses tell me everything, don't they?

To love the world is to love everything in it. This is not as easy as it sounds. Rare indeed is the person who can pull it off. There is always some aspect of What-Is that is extremely difficult if not impossible to accept. Contradictions, for example. Reality is chockful of contradictions, but we want everything to make perfect sense. Do you really believe that we will be able to make sense of the entire universe someday?

Does God exist or not? Is God transcendent or immanent? Is everything fundamentally material or spiritual? Is nature all there is, or is some other force hard at work in the universe? If you don't find this line of (un)reasoning repugnant, then you are sleepwalking. The logic used here is completely absurd, yet *this* is as close as we can ever get to comprehending What-Is. Every thought we have about it is speculation, peppered by passing glimpses of the Real that vanish the moment we *think* about what it is exactly that we are apprehending. How much easier it is to enshrine an idea and call that Truth than to open our minds to endless possibility.

An old man in an even older truck picked me up while I was hitchhiking one night, then left me in the middle of nowhere. The entire time we were together he asked me questions that I could not answer. Then he disappeared, leaving me to contemplate those questions while wandering about in the darkness. To this day, I still don't have the answers.

While roaming around an abandoned quarry, I see countless swirls etched into the stone beneath my feet. These swirls, I am told, are the fossils of marine creatures that lived hundreds of millions of years ago. These are my predecessors on this planet, my ancestors. How am I supposed to grasp this?

The swirl of gastropods etched in stone, the swirl of conical wildflowers, the swirl of hurricanes and galaxies... What goes around comes around. The universe, I am told, is an infinite sphere whose center is nowhere. Space curves back onto itself. The eternal return. If this isn't the divine manifest in nature, then what is?

It's simple really. To induce a mystical moment, all one has to do is remove oneself from time and space then apprehend What-Is without bias or expectation. It's as easy as making one's self disappear. The hard part is making sense of it afterward.

The rising sun is a promise of things to come. It is chockful of possibility. Forget about the supernatural; there is no limit to the *natural*. There is no limit to what Nature can do. Evolution is a constant unfolding. One can see that in the sun rising, which is different from what it was the last time it was seen. Every sunrise is a mystical moment, a fleeting glimpse of infinity.

Getting out of bed in the morning, my bones remind me that I'm getting older. We all know where this train of thought goes. Eventually, I won't be here. Yet *something* will be here. Something will always be here. That is the infinite. That is What-Is.

After publishing a book full of my clever words, I like to take a copy with me into the woods — the deeper the better. There I build a small fire and feed my literary accomplishment into it one page at a time. When I'm done, all that remains is a pile of ashes with a few words still showing. Then I use my hands to work this ash into the soil until there is nothing left but soil. That way I'm not fooled into thinking that any part of my precious self is immortal.

I am a part of nature. Or perhaps I should say, nature is all that I am. As I contemplate this, I begin to realize that I am a part of an eternal "I" that is far greater than myself. Yet my ego finds this notion as unfathomable as it is repugnant.

I do not completely accept the universe for what it is. As hard as I may try, I still can't go there. My love of nature isn't that great. I still hold back, clinging to an egotistical notion of what I am and what the world *should* be. I am godlike, I whisper to myself, in utter contempt for What-Is. Then I go about rearranging things, confident that I can make the world a better place. Then I make God in my own image so that I can reject it. That is my ultimate folly. I hope to abandon this ridiculous worldview and fully embrace Nature before I die. But I am only human.

Spirit exists in the atom, even though we are not aware of it. Energy is no illusion. Everything *moves*.

I call myself a philosopher because I *think* about What-Is. But thinking is not apprehending. I speculate about what transpires during mystical moments, but this is just me acting like a dog chasing its tail. Words only get in the way. Round and round I go…

A thousand-mile stare through the trees as a campfire snaps and crackles at my feet. A stream flows nearby, endlessly talking. A gust of wind brews up out of nowhere, then dissipates. The sky overhead is full of stars, reminding me that I inhabit a planet spinning on its axis, somewhere in the universe. Mine is an elemental existence. I am overwhelmed by it.

My biochemical reality leads me to believe that all living things can be reduced to their particulars, to cells, atoms, subatomic particles. All this is true, certainly, but it doesn't explain why we reproduce, why information passes from one life-form to another, or how this process first came about. Nor does it explain why *anything* is organized, let alone a complex, multicellular organism like me. And forget about consciousness. That makes no sense at all, arising as it has after billions of years of cosmic evolution, from what was once a completely inanimate universe.

Do rocks possess anything akin to consciousness? If not, then how did I come to be in what was once a completely inanimate universe? If so, then what are they thinking about on any given day? Whenever we mere mortals seriously think things through, we find ourselves thinking the unthinkable.

I am a thinking monkey, smarter than the average primate. But to think is to suffer, for I cannot think my way to a complete understanding of What-Is. Nature confounds me. It does not adhere to the logical rules of *my* way of thinking. Nature, it seems, has its own logic, where anything is possible.

Evolution is the most deeply religious concept that humankind has ever devised — a giant leap towards understanding the ways of Nature, the mind of God. Evolution suggests *duration*, the meaningful passage of time. This, in turn, suggests that Nature has some agenda unbeknownst to us. In our incredible arrogance, we deny this, simply because we are not privy to Nature's secrets. And in this denial, we deny What-Is.

Everything is random, some say, ignoring gravity. That and all the other laws of nature apply only to *this* universe, we are told. Other universes have other laws. Let's consider for a moment those other universes, where atoms never split, where stars are dark and cold, and things fall up when they are dropped. Let's imagine a universe where ten thousand frogs create a sacred text simply by jumping up and down on a keyboard, willy nilly. Go ahead and believe whatever you want to believe, ignoring What-Is. Be as utterly unscientific as you want to be in your scientific approach and see where that gets you. Then make yourself a campfire, paying close attention to what you are doing. What are you going to use for fuel? How are you going to ignite it? How do you keep it going or put it out?

I am wrong. You agree, I am wrong, thinking you are right. But you are also wrong. We are all wrong. We are all wrong because none of us has all the information about Nature, about What-Is. We think we have a good bead on things, but we are off the mark by more than we realize. Much more. A mystical moment makes this clear. When, for a split second, we sense What-Is, we see the error of our ways. Finding proof of this isn't difficult. All we have to do is get on the other side of denial, and there are our errors on full display. Then we know for a fact that our cosmological models are no more perfect than we are.

The universe is absurd because we are absurd. That is, we project our errors upon it, thinking Nature makes no more sense than we do simply because we cannot grasp it.

Seeing the trees is easy enough. Seeing the forest is much more difficult. The whole eludes us, especially when we get bogged down in the particulars. To see the whole, we must see in another way — in a way in which seeing goes beyond mere seeing.

How foolish am I, a thinking monkey, trying to see without seeing? At some point along the evolutionary path, my thinking has confounded me. I am now lost in my thoughts, speculating about the infinite, about What-Is, even though I haven't the slightest clue what it is that I am thinking about. *Homo absurdus*.

Tower of babel. There is the language of science. There are languages of religion and languages of philosophy. There are many other languages, as well — perhaps as many languages as there are those who speak. When we talk to each other, we speak in different languages. Quite often the true meanings of our words are untranslatable. Very little is communicated as a result. Very little is communicated, that is, except hard feelings. You don't understand me, I don't understand you, and we hate each other for it. How much easier it is to go to war than to talk to each other.

Any awareness of God is essentially self-awareness, for God is in all things, including us. Nature is in all things, that is. The force that drives all things is implicit in all things, that is. Information passes into us and through us, invigorating us and the entire universe.

Thinking, not thinking. Feeling, not feeling. Being, not being. There's no point trying to make sense of the world if you aren't willing to think, feel and be. Perhaps there is no point trying to make sense of the world at all. One can sleepwalk through life instead. But what's the point of that?

There are a thousand different ways for a human being to self-destruct, but none of them is quite as effective as denying one's all-too-human nature. Perhaps all self-destruction is rooted in that. The denial of human nature begins with the denial of Nature itself. Perhaps that is what's wrong with humankind as a whole.

I long for something I cannot see, hear, or touch. I long for something beyond my senses, while sensing that something else is going on in the universe. Correction: I *know* something else is going on in the universe, but I can't make sense of it. My thoughts, my beliefs are not enough. I go beyond them to apprehend What-Is. But whenever I do that, I remain just as clueless as I was before. Words fail me.

Immersed in a wild forest, I gradually release my own wildness from captivity. That is how I accept What-Is, or at least *think* I do. But I can't sustain this acceptance. Eventually, I leave the forest and interact with my own kind again. Then I am just as unaccepting as I was before. Denial, it seems, is contagious.

I move heaven and earth trying to understand What-Is, yet it remains elusive. I experience only brief apprehensions of it and have only wild speculations about what it is that I have just apprehended. Some critical aspect of What-Is always eludes me, as it eludes all seekers. Better to sleepwalk through life, some say, but I can't do that — not all the time, anyhow.

Once you have caught even the slightest glimpse of the infinite, there is no getting away from it. The desire to understand What-Is sticks to you like a bur, going with you wherever you go. Then comes another mystical moment and you are hopelessly engaged. Then you cannot walk away from What-Is without self-destructing.

God exists; God does not exist. What do we really mean when we utter the word "God" or the word "Nature" in our quest to understand things? Think about this. Think long and hard about this, then consider alternative words, alternative meanings. The infinite has infinite possibilities. What-Is has no bounds.

About the Author

Walt McLaughlin holds a degree in philosophy but insists that his thoughts regarding the relationship between God, nature and humankind have arisen largely from his backcountry experiences. He has been wondering, wandering, and writing for over 40 years. He has over twenty books in print, including a narrative about his immersion in the Alaskan bush, *Arguing with the Wind*, a collection of essays, *Cultivating the Wildness Within*, and a venture into religious philosophy, *A Reluctant Pantheism*. He is also the force behind a small press called Wood Thrush Books, through which he has selected and published the works of Ralph Waldo Emerson and other 19th Century nature writers, as well as contemporary ones. He lives in Swanton, Vermont with his wife, Judy.

For more information about Walt's books, visit the WTB website: **www.woodthrushbooks.com**

Go to **www.facebook.com\WaltMcLaughlin** to check out his Facebook page, or read his regularly posted blogs at **www.woodswanderer.com**

www.ingramcontent.com/pod-product-compliance
Lightning Source LLC
Chambersburg PA
CBHW022339280326
41934CB00006B/696